Fact Finders®

MEDIA LITERACY

YOURSPACE

Questioning New Media

by Heather E. Schwartz

Capstone
press®

Mankato, Minnesota

Fact Finders are published by Capstone Press,
151 Good Counsel Drive, P.O. Box 669, Mankato, Minnesota 56002.
www.capstonepress.com

Library of Congress Cataloging-in-Publication Data
Schwartz, Heather E.
    Yourspace : questioning new media / Schwartz, Heather E.
    p. cm. — (Fact finders. Media literacy)
    Summary: "Describes what media is, how new media is a part of the media, and
encourages readers to question the medium's influential messages" — Provided by publisher.
    Includes bibliographical references and index.
    ISBN-13: 978-1-4296-1993-6 (hardcover)
    ISBN-10: 1-4296-1993-7 (hardcover)
    1. Mass media — Juvenile literature. 2. Mass media — Influence — Juvenile literature.
I. Title.
P91.2.S39 2009
302.23 — dc22   2007050492

Editorial Credits

Jennifer Besel, editor; Juliette Peters, set designer; Kyle Grenz, book designer; Jo Miller,
    photo researcher

Photo Credits

All photos by Capstone Press, except:
AP Images/Stephan Savoia, 28 (right)
Courtesy of Heather E. Schwartz, 32
Photo Courtesy of Leonard Kleinrock, 28 (left)
Shutterstock/argus, 7, 13, 21 (background); Blazej Maksym, cover (computer); Elnur,
    cover (phone)

1 2 3 4 5 6 13 12 11 10 09 08

TABLE OF CONTENTS

iMEDIA

Take a look around your house. See the newspaper on the table? The TV in the living room? Newspapers and TV are part of the **media**. So are billboards, radio, and magazines. And today, there's also a whole category called new media.

New media includes things like wikis, podcasts, and social networking sites. It also includes technologies that haven't even been invented yet.

LINGO

wiki: server software that allows users to create and edit Web pages

New media is used to inform and entertain. And it's also used to **influence** us. That's why it is important to question the new media we use every day. Here are some questions to help you get started.

QUESTION IT!

Who made the message and why?

Who is the message for?

How might others view the message differently?

What is left out of the message?

How does the message get and keep my attention?

USERS 2.0

Who made the message and why?

People use new media for different reasons. Some people use new media to sell things. Others use it to inform and entertain.

Sometimes you may know why the message was made, but you don't know who made the message. Many new technologies allow users to remain **anonymous**. Have you ever gotten an IM from a stranger? Who knows what that person is up to?

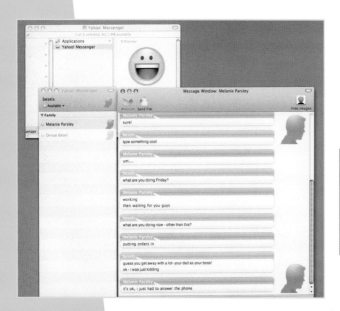

Instant messaging with friends is a lot of fun. But have you ever had a stranger try to IM you? Question those strange messages to keep yourself safe.

REALITY CHECK

Wikipedia is an online encyclopedia. Anyone can put information on the site. People can also make changes to posted information. Now, a new technology called Wikipedia Scanner can track who is making the changes. Virgil Griffith, a graduate student at the California Institute of Technology, created the scanner. With the scanner, people have found that millions of Wikipedia entries have been edited by corporations. Some drug companies are accused of deleting negative information about their medicines. This could be dangerous to people using the medicines.

WikiScanner: List anonymous wikipedia edits from interesting organizations

Now with mashable JSON!

by Virgil Griffith   v at santafe dot edu

[media ppl are required read this before asking questions]

Hello Wired, boingboing, Radar, Daily Kos, lgf, digg, /., Chronicle, Mashable, ValleyWag, Guardian, US News, BBC, Times Online, Planet Chiropractic, Le Monde, Der Spiegel, El Pais, Forbes, Daily Telegraph, CBS News, heise online, Linux Insider, New York Times, Int. Herald Tribune, pugbus, p2pnet, Penny Arcade, IT Blogwatch, HowStuffWorks, Time, Sydney Morning Herald, techtarget, The Onion, Slate, WikiNews, CMD readers / NPR, Radio Canada, BBC Radio5 listeners / Colbert Report, gnooze watchers!

WikiScanner is available for English, Nederlands, 中文, Polski, Italiano, Deutsch, Français, and 日本語 Wikipedia.

Specify by the Organization's...		Editor's Picks
Name:	<-- Type organization name here	Wired's list of salacious edits
		Submit a salacious edit
or / and		
		Lists
Location:	<-- Don't abbreviate here	Most common .gov's
		Most common .mil's
	Reveal my potential victims!	Most common .au's
		Most common .gov.au's
		Most common .uk's
		Most common .gov.uk's
OR		
		Government
Specify by Wikipedia page		U.S. Senate Sergeant At Arms
		U.S. House Of Representatives
Page Title	<-- Type a wikipedia article title here	Environmental Protection Agency
		National Institute of Health
	List Organizations	Democratic Party
		Republican Party
		Central Intelligence Agency
OR		
		Education
User-submitted Organizations		California Institute of Technology
		Bob Jones University
	Select IP range by owner	
		Policy
		Electronic Frontier Foundation

People all around the world use new media every day. Here are a few examples of why people create new media messages.

INDIVIDUALS create profiles on social networking sites. They stay connected with friends and meet new people.

CORPORATIONS use e-mail blasts to tell customers about new products or sales.

LINGO

blasts: sending information to a large mailing list at once

MUSICIANS create Web pages to showcase their music and promote upcoming concerts.

TV EXECUTIVES get viewers to watch shows by inviting them to text and play along.

MUSEUM DIRECTORS use podcasts to tell people about exhibits. They hope listeners will visit.

NONPROFIT ORGANIZATIONS use blogs to tell people about their cause.

YOU HAVE A MESSAGE

Who is the message for?

It takes time and money to create new media messages. Companies create messages with specific groups of people in mind. They use new media to convince their target audiences to buy their products. Companies target people of a certain age, gender, or income level. Imagine a bank offering credit cards to college students. It might send an e-mail blast to customers ages 18 to 22.

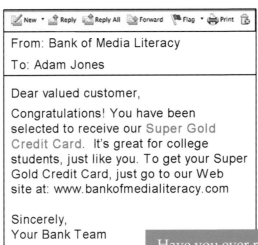

> New ▾ 📩 Reply 📩 Reply All 📤 Forward 🚩 Flag ▾ 🖨 Print 📇
>
> From: Bank of Media Literacy
> To: Adam Jones
>
> Dear valued customer,
> Congratulations! You have been selected to receive our Super Gold Credit Card. It's great for college students, just like you. To get your Super Gold Credit Card, just go to our Web site at: www.bankofmedialiteracy.com
>
> Sincerely,
> Your Bank Team

Have you ever received an e-mail trying to get you to buy something or visit a certain Web site? You were a part of someone's target audience.

Focusing In

Companies do research to find out what their audiences want. They use e-mail, IMs, and online surveys to get feedback from customers. In 2003, America Online (AOL) got information from customers online. AOL learned it needed better spam blockers. AOL fixed the problem and kept customers happy. In the process, more people started using AOL.

LINGO

target audience: the group of people that marketers think will be interested in their message

Write a script for a podcast about your favorite holiday. Your target audience is people who don't celebrate the holiday. As you write, think about these questions.

- How can you present the information in an interesting way?

- Will your podcast be for kids or adults?

- What does your target audience need to know about the subject?

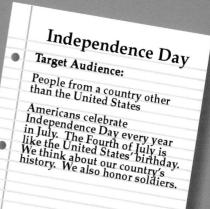

Independence Day

Target Audience:

People from a country other than the United States

Americans celebrate Independence Day every year in July. The Fourth of July is like the United States' birthday. We think about our country's history. We also honor soldiers.

11

Where Are You?

Companies also have to know how to reach their audiences. They can use new media for this purpose. All they need to do is ask customers for their cell phone numbers and e-mail addresses. Then the companies can reach people directly.

Popular Web sites and message boards are another way companies reach their audiences. They post information or buy ads on these sites. They'll use just about any form of new media to reach their audiences. Millions of young adults visit MySpace. That's why the U.S. Marine Corps created a profile on the site.

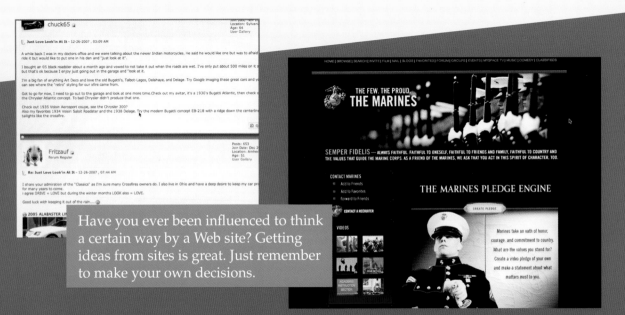

Have you ever been influenced to think a certain way by a Web site? Getting ideas from sites is great. Just remember to make your own decisions.

REALITY CHECK

Second Life is a virtual world online. People create an avatar who can hang out, go to parties, and shop. Companies learned shopping was popular in Second Life, so they brought their products there. American Apparel opened a virtual clothing store. Calvin Klein created a virtual perfume to sell. Coca-Cola even launched a contest to get players to design a virtual Coke machine. Why did real life companies want to get into Second Life? They realized this new media could be a great way to reach lots of real shoppers.

LINGO

avatar: a 3-D image used to represent someone online

VALUABLE TECHNOLOGY

How might others view the message differently?

What do you care about most? Your family? Your pets? Time off from homework? Values are the ideas you believe in. People have different values depending on their age, gender, and life experiences. Other factors also affect your values, such as where you live and how much money you have.

Your values can change too. Cool clothes or popular video games might be important to you now. But they might not be as important when you're 30.

Adults probably think the Cartoon Network Web site is silly. But you might fall asleep looking at the *Chicago Tribune* online. Values play a big part in what Web sites you visit too.

14

Values in Action

Values play a big role in how people view a new media message. You see, a message can be funny to one person but **offensive** to another. Imagine a wall post on Facebook that says, "Jen looks like a hippo." Some might think that sounds silly. But an overweight person might find it hurtful. No one views new media messages the same way.

Friends can view wall posts on each other's Facebook sites. Those posts could be funny to one person but hurtful to another.

15

The Freedom to Choose

People send millions of messages through new media devices. Those messages reflect millions of values. However, those values don't have to be yours. New media is a great way to get ideas. But you get to choose how you think and feel about those ideas.

Cyberbullies send new media messages that are meant to hurt others. Have you ever gotten a mass e-mail about someone? Then people teased that person because of the message they received? That e-mail showed the sender's values. But you don't have to think the same way.

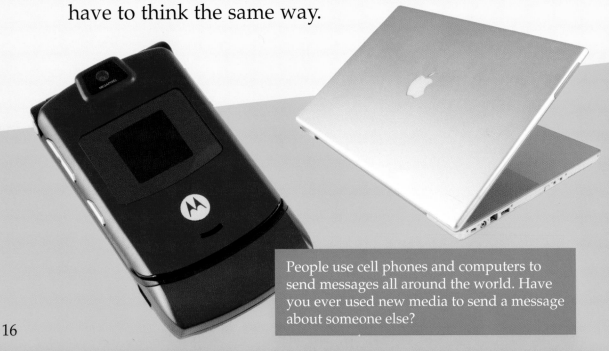

People use cell phones and computers to send messages all around the world. Have you ever used new media to send a message about someone else?

Know the Lingo

Not everyone views new media messages the same way. Older people didn't grow up with IMs and cell phones. Some people don't have money to buy new technology. They might not think new media is useful. Or they might not value the latest technology.

Media messages use language only their target audience understands. Do you know what these terms mean? Check your answers below. Then ask your friends, parents, and grandparents if they can define the terms. See who gets the most right.

DODGEBALL **PHISHING** **TEXT**

Answer Key

dodgeball: a social network that links your online friends to your cell phone

phishing: a scam designed to steal personal information about a user

text: another term for a text message, which is sent and received by cell phone

What is left out of the message?

Some new media messages are ads in disguise. For example, Nickelodeon aired Neopets Mini-Shows. These were fun to watch. But the shows were also designed to get viewers to use new Neopets products.

Do you think that the Mini-Shows on Nickelodeon made people more interested in Neopets products?

Should I Know That?

New media messages often leave out detailed instructions. Cell phone ads don't explain how to "text message." That can make you feel smart if you're tech-savvy. Or it can make you feel old-fashioned if you're not. Either way, the message makers are using your feelings to get you to buy their product.

Troublesome Tricks

Individuals can also use new media to their advantage. Take teens in Great Britain who wanted to use their cell phones in class. They found a way to get calls without teachers knowing. Mosquito is a high-pitched sound that adults can't hear. The sound was meant to drive teens away from storefronts. But teens found it made a great ringtone too. As long as teens kept the ringtone secret, they could use their phones in class.

Sneaky Surfers

Sometimes people use new media to harm or trick others. When that's the case, they're sure to keep information to themselves. It's easy for adults to pose as teenagers online. On networking sites like MySpace, some adults sign up using fake names and ages. You have to ask yourself why they would do that. And you also have to wonder if they have a criminal past.

Some new media is so new, it's impossible to control. New technology is fun and useful. But it's also used by a lot of people. And those people might not be telling the truth about who they are or what they want.

REALITY CHECK

In 2006, Megan Meier made a new friend on MySpace. A boy named Josh contacted her, and they began exchanging messages. After a month, Josh ended their friendship. He sent Megan messages saying cruel things about her. He also said he didn't want to be her friend. Megan was on medication for depression. Josh's actions hurt her a lot. The next day, Megan committed suicide.

After Megan's death, her parents learned something about the Josh on MySpace. Josh did not exist. Instead, Lori Drew and her daughter had created the profile. The women were Megan's neighbors. The women told police that they used the profile to learn what Megan said about them online.

This is an extreme example. But it happened. That's why it's important to beware of what new media messages might be leaving out.

Annie   Oct 16 2007 11:19 PM

kate!!! i heard you are coming home in a few weeks. yayayay!!! i miss you soo much. i hope school is fab and you haven't gotten kidnapped or anything yet. haha can't wait to see you!

Sarah*   Oct 16 2007 11:12 PM

just thought i'd let you know...yoyu are like a crazy person, arnie! :)

emma♥   Oct 14 2007 8:27 PM

i miss you stinky!!!

Marissa   Oct 11 2007 12:28 PM

Kate I miss you!!! How's school? When are you coming back to visit?

(gwen) STEFANI   Sep 22 2007 10:46 AM

sr year has been ok...i just want to go to college lol
i was thinking of going to the concert
and if i do ill def be sure to bring that pic of u lol

DOWNLOADABLE TRICKS

How does the message get and keep my attention?

New media messages are everywhere. In part, that's how new media gets your attention. Ads pop up when you log on to Web sites. Soda bottles give out free music downloads. Magazines ask you to text in codes. Those tricks definitely get your attention.

Do these things get your attention? The next time you see one of these tricks, pay attention to how you feel. Do you want to text in or click onto that site?

Mobi-What?

Some companies use sneakier ways to get your attention. Mobisodes might look like entertainment, but watch out. They also get you looking at commercials. Toyota sponsored two-minute mobisodes of the TV show *Prison Break*. Of course, each mobisode begins with a 10-second ad for Toyota's newest car.

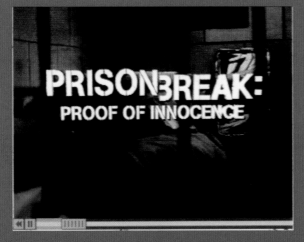

23

Hands-on Media Messages

There are lots of messages competing for your attention. New media makers know the more **interactive** the messages are, the better. That's why *Big Brother* viewers could vote back a housemate through text messaging. And *One Tree Hill* fans used texting to vote on what should happen in an upcoming show.

New video games are more interactive too. When you play Wii, you stand up and move around. It's as if you were really bowling or boxing. That's much more interesting than sitting on the couch pressing buttons.

Consumers can select the ending of a *One Tree Hill* episode via a text messaging campaign

Are interactive features interesting to you? Getting involved is fun. Just keep in mind that the message maker is trying to keep you interested so you'll keep coming back for more.

New and Better

Of course, new media products aren't new for long. Product developers keep creating new technologies to get our attention. And it works. When Apple came out with the iPhone, people couldn't wait to buy it. One million iPhones were sold in the United States in just 74 days.

Pretend you are a product developer. What kind of new media product would you like to invent? Consider these questions as you brainstorm:

- What do you wish you could do with new media products that can't be done today?
- Could you combine two or three new media products to create something new and exciting?

New Media Ideas

1. Put a printer inside a computer monitor, so paper comes out right under screen.

2. Make a cell phone into something people can wear, like a belt or headband.

3. Give cell phones a fold out screen, so people can see things bigger.

25

More, More, More

So you posted a video on YouTube. You're probably going to go back to see what people are saying, right? That's just one way new media keeps your attention. New media messages offer free downloads or contests. Then, they tell you to keep coming back for more free stuff or more chances to win.

Product developers work to make sure new media keeps your attention. When they create new products, they also develop additional equipment and software to go along with them. That way, customers won't get bored with products.

YouTube and the Wii game system are two popular forms of new media. And they both keep coming up with new ways to keep your attention. Do you think the Zapper is one of those ways?

Log Off

Can you escape new media messages? Probably not. But you don't need to. Keep questioning the new media messages around you. Then decide how you think and feel about the messages you're getting. So grab your latest gadget, and have fun finding the tricks in new media messages.

No matter what kind of new media you're using, remember to question those messages you're getting. You don't have to believe everything you see and hear.

TIME LINE

Four universities are connected through a computer system, beginning the Internet.

Tim Berners-Lee develops the World Wide Web.

1989

1972

1969

E-mail is introduced.

American Apparel opens a store in the virtual world Second Life. This move proves that companies are using new media to reach their target audiences.

1992

2006

2007

A mobile phone in the United Kingdom receives one of the first text messages.

Apple sells 1 million iPhones after 74 days on sale in the United States.

Virgil Griffith invents Wikipedia Scanner. It shows that companies change their entries to promote a positive image.

GLOSSARY

anonymous (uh-NON-uh-muhss) — written, done, or given by a person whose name is not known or made public

influence (IN-floo-uhnss) — to have an effect on someone or something

interactive (in-tur-AK-tiv) — allowing users to make choices in order to control something

media (MEE-dee-uh) — a group of mediums that communicates messages; one piece of the media, like new media, is called a medium.

offensive (uh-FEN-siv) — causing anger or hurt feelings

INTERNET SITES

FactHound offers a safe, fun way to find Internet sites related to this book. All of the sites on FactHound have been researched by our staff.

Here's how:

1. Visit *www.facthound.com*

2. Choose your grade level.

3. Type in this book ID **1429619937** for age-appropriate sites. You may also browse subjects by clicking on letters, or by clicking on pictures and words.

4. Click on the **Fetch It** button.

FactHound will fetch the best sites for you!

READ MORE

Ali, Dominic. *Media Madness: An Insider's Guide to Media*. Tonawanda, N.Y.: Kids Can Press, 2005.

Wan, Guofang. *Virtually True: Questioning Online Media*. Media Literacy. Mankato, Minn.: Capstone Press, 2007.

Woodford, Chris. *Digital Technology*. Science in Focus. New York: Chelsea House, 2006.

INDEX

MEET THE AUTHOR

Heather E. Schwartz started questioning new media when she learned she'd need to buy new software in order to get the most out of her new laptop computer. Heather has taught media literacy workshops for girls ages 9 to 14 and developed media literacy curriculum for Girls Inc. of the Greater Capital Region, a local site of the national nonprofit youth organization.